NORI

THE STORY of a DEAF HONDURAN ORPHAN and the

GOODNESS of
GOD

Robert K. Rittenhouse

2013

AuthorHouse™
1663 Liberty Drive
Bloomington, IN 47403
www.authorhouse.com
Phone: 1-800-839-8640

Published by AuthorHouse 01/18/2013

ISBN: 978-1-4772-8057-7 (sc)
978-1-4772-8058-4 (e)

Library of Congress Control Number: 2012919270

Any people depicted in stock imagery provided by Thinkstock are models,
and such images are being used for illustrative purposes only.
Certain stock imagery © Thinkstock.

This book is printed on acid-free paper.

Because of the dynamic nature of the Internet, any web addresses or links contained in this book may have changed since publication and may no longer be valid. The views expressed in this work are solely those of the author and do not necessarily reflect the views of the publisher, and the publisher hereby disclaims any responsibility for them.

Note from the author: Nearly all of the pictures are pictures of our family members and the handful that include school pictures, permission is also granted. The school pictures are covered by a blanket permission given by parents.

Bible Citations: The NIV Topical Study Bible (1989)
Zondervan Bible Publishers
Grand Rapids, Michigan

authorHOUSE®

TABLE of CONTENTS

DEDICATION

"Nori" is dedicated to Nori's mother and my wife, Patricia Kenyon Rittenhouse. While Pat will tell you that many, many people have made important contributions to Nori's adoption and her successes (and many have), Pat was always there teaching, helping, encouraging, nurturing our daughter. Pat never once shirked the responsibility she had assumed. She is a remarkable woman who never seeks recognition and always gives the ultimate credit where it belongs: with God.

Pat with Nori at age eight

ACKNOWLEDGEMENTS

Carlos Zuniga of Tegucigalpa, the founder of Centro de Vida and Alan Danforth (now deceased), the Founder of World Gospel Outreach in Tegucigalpa, Honduras.

John and Joy White AND Ernie and Barbara (now deceased) Northup of Fellowship Bible Church in Little Rock.

Linda Johnson and Christine Fahrenbruch, Nori's first teachers, Susan Pack and Mike Phillips, Nori's first Superintendent and Principal AND Stacey Tatera, the Director of Singing Fingers where Nori got her "performing" experience, all from the Arkansas School for the Deaf.

Jean, David and Noel King, Nori's "second family" in Little Rock, Dr. Gene Campbell (now deceased), my Dean at the University of Arkansas-Little Rock AND our adoption lawyer in Little Rock.

Pat McAnally, former Director of Education at the Arizona School for the Deaf who was instrumental in Nori's transfer at a time when Nori still had immigrant status only.

Carol LaCava and Kim Hinchey of Interact in Knoxville where Nori was introduced to professional acting AND Jerry Seale, Nori's Knoxville Pastor who baptized Nori.

Sallee Reynolds, Nori's principal at West who believed in Nori right from the beginning and was her biggest supporter, Patsy Lowe her supervising teacher and Chris Kessler her basketball coach who got her into the game every chance he got.

Laurie Mosely of the National Technical Institute for the Deaf who guided Nori's academic program and kept her on track for graduation AND Mindy Hopper her NTID "sister" and Marilyn Mitchell her NTID "aunt" who helped keep her on track and out of "trouble".

Paul and Mindy Brouse of the Texas Lions Camp who provided the internship while Nori was at NTID that changed her direction in life.

Chrissy Moreno and Dr. Bob Weinstock at Gallaudet who helped her succeed, Dr. Alan Hurwitz, the Gallaudet President who helped Nori with admission to the University AND Mikaela Hudson, her track coach at Gallaudet who always encouraged her.

Anne Green, my one and only niece, for her help on proofing and making editing suggestions.

REFLECTIONS on NORI

I was first introduced to Nori Rittenhouse when she auditioned to be in a play with InterAct Children's Theatre for the Deaf. I had worked with deaf actors and with fresh faced kids in the past but something about Nori was different. She seemed quiet and reserved but willing to learn. She was so serious about getting into her character and learning her lines that she was getting frustrated and I was afraid she would quit. At one point, I told her to "do what I do" and began acting silly. Her eyes grew wide, her mouth went slack and she signed, "Really? Just like that?" and I nodded. A huge grin came over her face and she proceeded to act like the biggest goofball you had ever seen. Her laugh and good spirit was infectious. She was a great actress and we became fast friends. In one play, I spoke the lines that she would sign. I became her "voice." As proud as I was of her acting, my heart swelled with pride when she was named Valedictorian from her high school. Listening to her speech at graduation, I knew Nori would continue to go far. Having seen the actual disparity in Tegucigalpa, I know that Nori (with the help of a loving family and group of friends) had already overcome so much. Now it is her turn to be the "voice" of others. And a mighty voice, that will be.

-Kim Hinchey, CT/CI and NIC
Certified Sign Language Interpreter

On a trip back from Camp Caraway, a Christian Camp for youth in North Carolina, Nori and I began to chat. When I shared with Nori that I too was adopted, an instant bond formed between us that remains strong today. At the time Nori was 14 years old and was beginning to question life. Over the years, we have had many good conversations about our shared adoptions and many other things important to each of us. I think the world of Nori. One of Nori's big concerns that once even brought her to tears was the rejection she felt at being left alone in Honduras. We talked about that at length and how we are all adopted as God has adopted all of us into His family. I shared with Nori that she was blessed to be adopted by Bob and Pat, that she was chosen. Nori was comforted by our conversations and by this new perspective. I am so proud of what Nori has done in her young life and what she has become. Nori is a Doer and that makes her very special to the Deaf Community. I know Nori that you are going to make the world a better place for young deaf children and their families through your work upon your graduation from Gallaudet University. Go soar Nori.

-Phil Beam of Knoxville, Tennessee
Nori's Deaf brother in Christ

Nori and I met at the National Technical Institute for the Deaf (NTID), at the Rochester Institute of Technology (RIT) in 2007. Nori was majoring in Arts and Imaging Studies and I became her assigned counselor/academic advisor. Nori was such a joy to work with. She was very sweet, gentle, and caring and a bundle of energy. I also discovered that she had a very stubborn part to her. She was very determined to reach her goals and to reach them in her own way.

As part of my job, I tried to learn more about Nori's background, however, Nori was not interested in reliving her past. Nori showed appreciation for her parents for adopting her from Honduras, and being there for her however she resisted questions about her past. I asked her why. Nori shared that while growing up, she received lots of attention through articles and interviews related with her adoption. Nori also shared that she really wanted to get away from all that and be recognized for who she was now, and be her own person. She said someday she probably will be more open to talking about her past again, but for now, she was more focused on trying to find the person that she was trying to become.

Finding that person included trying to figure out what she wanted to do with her life. In 2009, during a conversation with Nori, she shared her excitement about a required co-op field experience where she worked at a camp with special needs children. she was to be their photographer. She loved her internship. She said that she now knew what she wanted to do. She wanted to combine her skills in photography and work with special needs children.

In 2010, Nori graduated with an associates degree from NTID/RIT and made plans to transfer to Gallaudet University. English was not easy for Nori; she did not pass the necessary English tests to be accepted directly into the bachelor program. Nori's stubbornness surfaced: she was determined to study at Gallaudet University. She worked hard to improve her English. Her dad, Bob, shared with me recently that Nori was fully accepted into the bachelors degree program at Gallaudet University! I must say, I was not surprised at all! Nori is very determined and I am very excited to see what she does next!

-Laurie Mosely, Advisor at the National Technical Institute for the Deaf Rochester Institute of Technology, Rochester, NY

Nori has a fascinating background, given her strong Honduran cultural roots and identity while being adopted by wonderful parents from the U.S., who deeply cared about her journey, learning about life. Nevertheless, Nori, from within herself, "gets it" more than many others. It's amazing how she did it arriving in the United States without any formal language, but with a hunger to learn. Credit must go to her Honduran birth family whose priority was to give Nori hope through adoption that was limited in Honduras. And credit her adoptive parents, Pat and Bob, for providing her with a good and loving home with accessible language. Accessible language, at home, is so foundational to learning and developing in all aspects of life. But ultimately, I give credit to Nori for her resiliency and her un-stoppable ambition to learn and become independent. By navigating through her own journey of life, including making good decisions while taking risks, she has arrived. It's her Deafhood and her Honduranhood journeys that will now take her afar. I so enjoyed being her big sister for three years. Onward and upward Nori.

-Mindy Hopper, Ph.D.
NTID, Rochester NY

There comes a time when each of us must decide to heed God's call to action and join Him in His divine work. This is the story of Bob and Pat's answer to that call. True religion, as defined by Scripture, is "to visit orphans and widows in their trouble, and to keep oneself unspotted from the world" (James 1:27, NKJV). Taking this verse to heart, the Rittenhouses decided to open their hearts and home to a deaf child. In His mysterious but wonderful way, God brought Nori and the Rittenhouses together. What follows is the journey that Bob, Pat, and Nori traveled as they became a family. It is a beautiful story of God's grace and love. Having known the Rittenhouses for a number of years, I can attest to the blessing that Bob and Pat have been to Nori as well as the blessing Nori has been to each person she meets. May God use this book to challenge each of us to answer His call and show His love in a world that is in such desperate need.

-Charles W. Penland Jr. D.Min.
Kirby Woods Baptist Church, Memphis

INTRODUCTION

I was a single father when I met my future wife Pat Kenyon or Patty as I call her. We met in the fall of 1984 and I was raising my two daughters Julie (age 18 at the time) and Nancy who was 16. They had come to live with me following my divorce when they were seven and five years old. In that fall of 1984 I was a full professor and Director of Deaf Education at Illinois State University. Pat was a student there having just transferred from the University of Illinois. Three years later, after a two-year courtship, we were married in my backyard. And a week later we were on our way to Little Rock, Arkansas where I again was a full professor and Patty was a middle school language arts teacher at the Arkansas School for the Deaf. I thought it was especially "neat" that Pat was taking the teaching position of Emogene Nutt who was retiring. Emogene was the wife of Houston Nutt, one of the most famous deaf athletes of all time and the father of the college football coach by the same name. What a nice "coincidence" as I was a true lover of sports myself.

Growing up in Rushville, Illinois I lived and breathed sports. Organized sports, pick-up games, sand-lot games, anything-anywhere games occupied most of my time. My teachers would even complain to my parents that the only books I read were sports books. I must have read the Babe Ruth story so many times, I had become a local expert on his life. **It didn't escape me that The Babe was an orphan.** Baseball and football, especially baseball, were my best and favorite sports and I played shortstop on the baseball team and quarterback on my high school football team, the Rushville Rockets.

The world we lived in in those days (the 1950s and early 60s), in small towns, where sports were what we lived for, we boys all dreamed of someday playing ball on the big stage. After all if Mickey Mantle, one of my boyhood idols, from a small town in Oklahoma could play centerfield for the New York Yankees, we could make it too. However my biggest stage was to play four years of varsity baseball for Illinois College, a small, private college in Jacksonville, right next to the Illinois School for the Deaf. I never met the Mick nor saw him play.

While a student at IC, I began working part-time for room and board at the Illinois School for the Deaf. It was 1964 and until my retirement in 2011, I have worked with the Deaf in one capacity or another my entire professional career. My family thought it "coincidental" that I made the Deaf my life's work. They told me stories about my grand mother Tressa, who died before I was born, and her relationship with the Deaf in Rushville. My grand mother was a very strong Christian woman and each Sunday she would minister to the Deaf. They would come to church in Rushville in horse-drawn buggies from surrounding areas and Grandma would "interpret" the service for them and then make sure they participated in after-church activities. No one could remember Grandma ever learning sign language so they didn't know how she had learned to communicate with the Deaf. I suspect she used "home signs" and gestures and with her big heart a bond developed between Grandma and the Deaf. So here in 1987, I married a deaf woman who was taking the place of the wife of an iconic deaf sports figure at a school for the Deaf. It was as if I had "inherited" my love for the Deaf from my grand mother Tressa. A few days after school started, I met Houston Nutt when I drove onto the ASD campus. We had never met, but he knew who I was. When I got out of my car, he waved and said "Dr. Rittenhouse, how are you buddy". That was Houston! We became instant and life long friends until Houston's death in 2005. And when you were a friend of Houston's, you knew what true friendship meant.

Bob, Pat and Nori

I am one who has come to believe that there are very few (if any) "coincidences" in life. As my mother Evelyn Rittenhouse would always say, "things happen for a reason". Soon after arriving in Little Rock, we joined Fellowship Bible Church which had a Deaf Ministry led by a special couple, John and Joy White. The lead Sign Language Interpreter at the church was Barbara Northup, a hearing woman married to a deaf man named Ernie Northup. We became involved in the Deaf Ministry and got to know John and Joy and Barbara and Ernie very well. Barbara and Ernie had just taken a young, deaf child into their care who was from Tegucigalpa, Honduras. Her name was Aura. How wonderful of the Northups to so unselfishly help this young deaf child from such a poor country......

As I reflected on life after Nori's arrival in our family, I began to see the wisdom of my mother's faith that "things happen for a reason". My heart began to soften, my eyes began to see more clearly. In July of 1990 I had become born-again in a very profound way when my new son-in-law Cory died tragically. In trying to cope with his death and my daughter Julie's grief, I reached out to our Lord and Savior, Jesus Christ. He was right there for me; He had always been right there. No longer did some things happen by chance or coincidence; God was charting a path for me, a crooked path that He made straight through forgiveness, second chances and complete faithfulness. Indeed He had a plan for me....but what?

I believe that a very big part of God's plan involved a young deaf child from a very poor area of the world upon whom He poured out His goodness. And the young child named Nori responded to His favor by growing in to a beautiful young woman who, through His grace, has excelled. It is also the story of how God uses each of us, if we bend to His will, as His emissaries. **This is Nori's story.**

THE EARLY AMERICAN YEARS

Then I heard the voice of the Lord saying "Whom shall I send? And who will go for me?" And I said "Here am I. Send me". Isaiah 6:8

MY WIFE PAT'S MAIDEN TRIP TO HONDURAS

"By the way, my husband and I are interested in adopting a deaf child." With that, the adventure had begun. Little did we know how life changing the adoption of Nori Oyuki Barahona Burgos would be. My wife Pat was on a one-week mission trip to Tegucigalpa, Honduras with church friends from Little Rock ostensibly to assist American doctors and dentists there. This was my wife's first mission trip. Reluctantly she had agreed to accompany her friend Joy White. Pat is deaf and venturing into non-signing environments is always done with some nervousness. However Joy was a good signer and promised to interpret when Pat needed help communicating. So off they flew with a team to Tegucigalpa, Honduras in the heart of Central America.

It was February of 1996 and Pat, a teacher, had been given a week off to make the trip. I stayed home to hold down the fort. As a University Professor I had some flexibility in my schedule, but was teaching a full load that semester and decided to stay back. One week without Pat and then life would be back to normal. Only on reflection did we realize that the Lord wanted Pat in Tegucigalpa, not to help doctors and dentists, but to meet Nori. And little did I know that our life was about to be changed in a dramatic way.

A few days into her missionary work Pat was told that there was a man named Carlos who had recently started a church ministry for the Deaf of Honduras. This man also reached out to street children, sometimes finding orphans and bringing them to live at the World Gospel Outreach Centro de Vida orphanage. A thought came to mind: maybe this man Carlos had encountered deaf street children.

13

On Wednesday night, two days before Pat was scheduled to return to Little Rock, she and Carlos met at the headquarters of World Gospel Outreach, high on a mountain overlooking Tegucigalpa, Honduras' capitol. Carlos was no ordinary man. He was the only living son of a former Vice President of Honduras and had inherited the beautiful mansion of his family that was now home to World Gospel Outreach (WGO). Carlos' parents were now deceased and his only brother had been assassinated during the bloody Contra-Sandinista war. Carlos had become a born-again Believer, a Christian, only recently. He served as a consultant to WGO and in the evenings he would sit in and listen to the reflections shared by the missionaries from the day's work in the mission field that was Tegucigalpa.

Nori with Carlos in Tegucigalpa

After becoming born-again, Carlos spent three days in deep prayer and fasting. During this time, he came across the verse in the Bible that says that **"faith comes by hearing and hearing by the Word of God" (Romans 10:17).** His immediate thought upon reading this was, what about the Deaf? Although he had never personally met a deaf person, he felt a deep concern for them. His logical, engineering mind questioned how God would never block the pathway to Heaven for anyone, certainly not the Deaf. Inspired and challenged, he decided to seek out and help the Deaf of Tegucigalpa.

The first Deaf Honduran that Carlos encountered and befriended was Efrain Aguilar. Efrain took the time to introduce Carlos to other deaf people, and to teach Carlos Honduras Sign Language (LESHO). Slowly, Carlos became known in the deaf community of Tegucigalpa, and he was able to begin a church for them. At the same time, he was visiting other churches and sharing about his new ministry, in hopes of getting some financial support and also finding more deaf people.

On the Wednesday that Carlos and Pat met, it just so happened that the previous Sunday he had visited a church and spoke about the new deaf ministry. Afterwards, a lady in the congregation stood up and said, "I know a little deaf girl who has been abandoned. She lives with different families on a rotating basis". The lady explained that the girl played in the streets everyday while all the other children were at school. She knew this was not a safe situation, and wondered if Carlos could do anything for her. Carlos agreed to check into possible resources, took the lady's contact information and left.

That Wednesday night, he and my wife Pat talked for several hours as Carlos threw questions at Pat about teaching and working with the Deaf and Pat in turn shared ideas with Carlos. As they were about to end their conversation, Pat said the words that would turn our lives in a new and challenging direction: **"By the way, my husband and I are interested in adopting a deaf child".** God has an almost magical way of putting people and events together to help us in our time of need, especially "the least of us". Nori was not "the least" but at that time in her young life her future sure looked dark and uncertain. With God's Hand of Favor placed on her (and us) all that changed. In the next few chapters, you will see how our adventure became a love story. And to God we give all the Glory.

NORI

I will not leave you as an orphan; I will come to you. John 14:18

Nori Oyuki Barahona Burgos was born December 5, 1988 in Tegucigalpa, Honduras. Her mother Onilda was an older woman and her biological father was never in the picture. When Nori was three years old, her mother moved permanently to Miami and left Nori behind with her older sisters who were themselves adults. They too had immigrated to Miami but returned to Tegucigalpa for long visits. When her sisters were out of the country, which was often and for long stretches of time, Nori would be placed with different families. Tegucigalpa and all of Honduras was at that time almost completely lacking in education services for deaf children. Only those from wealthy families received an education and the instruction is what we would call here in the United States, home schooling. As Nori grew older she began to act out, wanting desperately to communicate. Carlos' vision of an orphanage-school for the Deaf offered a ray of hope. When Carlos met Pat that Wednesday night he recognized right away that God was at work, that He seemed to be putting into place His people in support of his/Carlos' vision. Carlos was moved.

Carlos was especially excited at Pat's comment about adoption and asked her if he could come back in an hour and bring Nori with him. He left the WGO in a dash and in less than an hour he was back with a very young, seven-year-old little girl with big brown eyes. Pat fell in love with Nori on the spot. It was 10 o'clock at night, much too late for a seven year old to be up but Nori and Pat "talked" to each other for over an hour. It was clear to Pat that Nori was bright, settled and composed, a child of God wanting to learn and become the special person God intended her to be. Word spread fast the next day among the missionaries that Pat had met Nori and that Nori was a young deaf child with endearing qualities. That day, which was now Friday the day before Pat was to return to the states one of the missionaries called his wife in Little Rock to tell her of Pat's "find". The wife happened to be a teacher at the school where Pat also taught. She in turn told her friend Libby Adamson who just happened to be one of my staff members and Libby came to my office and said "congratulations". Much to my surprise and somewhat shock I learned through the grapevine that stretched from Central America to the University of Arkansas in Little Rock by way of Libby that I was about to become an adoptive father of a deaf, Honduran child. Surprised because I didn't realize that adoption was on Pat's "agenda" and shocked because I had recently become a grand father.

Nori at the orphanage in Tegucigalpa

My grand daughter Hailey Varner had just entered the world and I had big hopes and dreams for her. After a few minutes as the news began to sink in, I started to wonder: "is this for real", "is it a little boy or little girl", "will she or he be with Pat tomorrow when the plane lands". That this was part of God's plan did not enter my mind at that time. The next day Pat arrived and I picked her up at the airport. Nori was not with her but there was plenty of excitement in the air. Pat couldn't stop talking about Nori on the way home and I couldn't stop thinking "this too will pass". It didn't of course and I thank the Good Lord everyday that it didn't. The next few months were to be challenging, difficult and often frustrating but we stayed the course in our efforts to bring Nori to Little Rock in time to start school at the Arkansas School for the Deaf that coming fall of 1996.

It is important here to say a little about Nori's homeland. Her biological family was a good family. Because of the harshness of Tegucigalpa (Honduras is the poorest country in Central America and considered to be one of the most dangerous places in the world), her family decided to move to Miami. The move took place covertly. Nori was left behind with friends and neighbors at the age of four. She was handed from family to family and was on balance, well cared for. Then along came Carlos and the orphanage. The orphanage provided her with a structured place to live and a social group (although all of the girls were considerably older than Nori). The orphanage also had a "school" and Nori was enrolled there for a few months before coming to the States with us. In fact, through the efforts of Carlos, Nori was enrolled while we were there in May. It touched our hearts so to see Nori sitting in class in her pretty white dress doing her best to learn. She couldn't hear (all of the other girls could) and she had no language, but she had heart. The one sign she did know was **I Love You**. We would stand outside the open classroom and watch her and she would turn and sign **ILY** to us and smile that beautiful Nori smile. My wife, ever the teacher, would sign back "pay attention" and Nori would snap right back to attention. We love the people of Tegucigalpa and have nurtured in Nori love and respect for them and for her family. Pat is on the board of directors of the new Happy Hands School for the Deaf (Manos Felices) there and travels to Tegucigalpa nearly every summer. This past summer we both traveled there. Nori hopes to do one of her Gallaudet field experiences at the school.

NORI HEADS TO LITTLE ROCK, ARKANSAS

The Lord will guide you always; He will satisfy your needs in a sun-scorched land and will strengthen your frame. You will be like a well watered garden, like a spring whose waters never fail. Isaiah 58:11

Bringing Nori to Little Rock was a very bumpy ride for us. We told Alan Danforth the head of World Gospel Outreach of our desire to bring Nori to Little Rock and start her in school and if at all possible to adopt her. Alan was all for it and dedicated himself along with Carlos, who now worked for World Gospel Outreach, to the plan. At the same time, a political campaign was being waged in the United States and one of the popular candidates was Pat Buchanan. Pat was a limited-immigrant candidate who was proposing that the US build a wall around its southern border. That notion was catching on, particularly in the south and tighter immigration guidelines were being drawn up in Washington. Alan learned as he began to make contacts for us in Tegucigalpa that foreign adoptions were now very difficult to achieve. The Honduran Government had learned that Americans prized their orphans and strict adoption laws had been passed making adoption difficult and expensive. As we navigated the roadblocks that we faced both here and in Honduras it became clear, in view of restrictions on both sides of the border, that bringing Nori to Little Rock in time for the start of school was possible only if we brought her here as an exchange student. In June of that year, my Dean, Dr. Gene Campbell, suggested that I travel to Tegucigalpa to do some workshops on deafness to teachers there. And Dean Campbell's "suggestions" were not to be taken lightly: "Rittenhouse, those teachers need your help" (Dr. Campbell called all of the professors by their last name, lest we become too taken by ourselves). But I knew she meant, "that little girl needs a family".

Our church, Fellowship Bible Church, had started a mission program in Tegucigalpa and so Pat and I collaborated with them and traveled to Tegucigalpa for two weeks in May of 1996. If there had been any doubt in my mind about the wisdom of adopting Nori (and there had been) it melted away after meeting her. In fact I decided then and there that nothing was going to stand in the way of that adoption. We had a wonderful two weeks there doing workshops with Brad and Helen Carlson and spending time with Nori. While she had no formal language whatsoever, she picked up on everything quickly and in her own way communicated with the other older orphans. As a university professor in the field of deafness, I had developed an eye for ability in deaf children and it was clear to me that she was full of talent and potential. But the big event there for me was of the heart and not the mind: I was brought to tears everyday with the new understanding that God's Hand of Favor had been placed squarely on what we were doing. The next couple of months we worked hard from our end and Alan and Carlos worked hard from their end to clear the way for Nori to come to Little Rock and start school at the Arkansas School for the Deaf. Everyone at school was excited at the prospect, as were the missionaries in Tegucigalpa. Would Nori make it? How would she take to Little Rock and her "new family"? What did God have in store?

Nori upon arrival at the Little Rock Airport

Nori arrived in Little Rock on the Friday before school registration on Monday. But her arrival was anything but smooth or certain. Her trip was to take place in early July when a missionary team was to fly from Tegucigalpa to Houston with Nori in tow. We had gathered around our kitchen table in Little Rock with our friends Barbara and Ernie Northup. They had pioneered the sponsorship of deaf children from Honduras by bringing Aura; a young deaf child from Tegucigalpa to Little Rock and Aura was flourishing at the Arkansas School for the Deaf. Nori would be the second deaf child from Honduras. As we waited for the phone to ring, Ernie, a deaf man, prayed for a safe flight. The phone rang, I answered it and delivered the bad news. Nori was not passed through security in Tegucigalpa. She wouldn't be coming. We all cried, especially my wife Pat. Soon we heard from Alan who said that there was some paperwork that had to be cleared up and he would send her on the next missionary trip to the states. The next Saturday, we once again gathered at the kitchen table, with great anticipation but also with worry. We had not yet placed the full challenge of getting Nori to Little Rock on our Lord and we were nervous. "Ring, ring, ring". It was Alan. He was at the airport and had personally escorted Nori to the plane bound for Houston. He handed Nori over to a missionary who had taken her hand and they had boarded. We could hardly contain our joy! The plane was still on the runway and Alan had returned to the waiting area to watch it depart. Then, "Hold on" he said. "Nori is getting off the plane". She was escorted back to Alan; once again the plan was aborted. The tears flowed at the kitchen table. Doubt began to sink in.

Soon thereafter Alan called to say that there had been a misunderstanding and he would try to clear that up and get Nori scheduled with the next team. The next Saturday, two days before school registration, we once again gathered in our kitchen, holding hands and praying. The call came, she was on the plane, she was sitting next to a missionary, the plane was jettising down the tarmac, it was airborne, Nori was Houston-bound. We were overcome with tears, but these tears were tears of joy and thanksgiving…the Lord had come through. We jumped in the car and drove to the Little Rock airport where Pat caught a flight to Houston to meet Nori. They would return to Little Rock that night.

We wonder what must have been going through Nori's mind. With no language to mediate her thoughts, her anticipations **AND** with little worldly experience, was she fearful? Excited? Confused? We'll never know. We are confident though that when God's Hand of Favor is upon you, you are certainly safe and may even sense internally that all is well. Nori seemed to be completely at ease and showed no reservations about leaving Tegucigalpa, her only home up to that time, and board a plane with strangers, heading for where she knew not. Pat said that it was chaotic at the large Houston Hobby Airport. But she found Nori without any trouble and Nori, holding onto the hand of a missionary, was all smiles. To this day, travel by car or air all over the United States is just no big deal to her. Her "little Gramma", my mother, would brag to anyone who would listen at what a brave, little traveler Nori was. We still marvel at her fearlessness.

LITTLE ROCK, ARKANSAS

Your hands made me and formed me; teach me to understand your commands. Psalm 119:73

Nori Oyuki Barahona Burgos arrived in Little Rock to a crowd of new friends and family. As I was walking the long gateway to the gate where Nori and Pat were arriving, I looked up at the departure and arrival electronic directory that hung from the ceiling. Next to their flight it said "on time". Tears welled up in my eyes, as I knew that it was God's way of saying that we were on "His time", that she arrived when she was supposed to and the delay and false starts only served to strengthen our faith in the Lord and His power. As I was to come to understand later, it was also meant to say, "be patient, things will turn out just fine, My Hand of Favor is upon you".

Nori and Pat walked from the plane, which had landed about 50 yards from the entrance, to the building. They were hand-in-hand. Nori was carrying a little suitcase that little girls use when they are playing dolls. All of her worldly possessions were in that little suitcase. She had a big smile on her face. Pat stopped and pointed up at all of us standing in the airport window waving. She waved and signed the **I Love You** sign that has become a universal sign. It is made by extending your thumb, index finger and little finger and folding your other two fingers into the palm of your hand. The little finger signifies I, the thumb and index finger form an L for Love and the thumb and little finger (and a now folded index finger) form a Y for You. When she stepped inside, about 40 people from our church, Fellowship Bible Church, were there to greet her. She looked around in awe and then spotted me. She dropped her suitcase and ran and jumped into my arms. I felt a sense of true joy that God's Goodness had brought her not just to Little Rock but also into my arms. Nori for her part signed ILY to everyone over and over. Noel, another little deaf child from China who had been adopted by a deaf couple, David and Jean King, and Nori curiously checked each other out. They were the same age and the same size and I think they recognized "who" they were. Noel was very bright and had learned American Sign Language. She put her arms around Nori and began signing to her. Nori responded with gestures. While she didn't understand what Noel had said, she clearly understood the meaning behind the signs: "WELCOME to LITTLE ROCK, Nori". We drove home and introduced Nori to her new home, her dog Leon, her bed and bedroom. She seemed to feel at home immediately.

What is it that allows a child to brush off the fear that can accompany such dramatic life change? It's God's Goodness. That night we stood at Nori's bunk bed and prayed with her. We used a gestural form of communication to introduce her to God that night, to thank Him for Nori's safe trip to Little Rock, to thank Him for loving Nori and asking Him to watch over her. It was a short prayer. Little did we know that in the weeks and months to come, the evening prayer would sometimes last an hour or more. And Nori was doing the praying. She would relive her day, every little detail and thank God ("Thank You God") for everything that she did that day. Her prayers became known in our family as "Nori's A-Z prayers".

On Sunday morning we were all up early getting ready to take Nori to the Arkansas School for the Deaf to register for school. Registration was in the gym and tables had been set up where the students and their parents signed up for various activities such as sports or clubs and where they filled out forms. It seemed that everyone was curious about Nori. She had a charisma about her even at the age of seven. Her teachers hugged her and introduced her around and Nori absorbed it all. There was no fear or shyness to be seen that morning. It was if she knew she belonged. She ran everywhere and met other deaf children without any hesitation. She was curious and would try to engage the other students, "helping" them communicate with her. She would show them her books, "comment" on their clothes. As I watched I felt that Nori seemed to be the returning student and had named herself the official welcoming committee. Pat, as a teacher at the same school, was busy with her registration responsibilities in another building so I was with Nori. It was a whirlwind of a day and the school was so good about "cutting corners" so that Nori could start right away even though she did not have some of the required paperwork. First on the list were vaccinations…and she didn't even have a doctor. Having arrived only 36 hours earlier, we were missing several things. However, Nori was cleared to start classes the next day. What a school!

Registration lasted most of the day and Nori loved every minute of it. She almost immediately identified with the other deaf children. The teachers all signed and they gave Nori a lot of extra attention. She was about as happy as a child could be…and school hadn't even started. I scheduled her with a doctor who was taken by her story and Nori would then begin what every child in America goes through: a round of shots that none look forward to. That afternoon we returned home and Joy, Pat's friend from church, came over to say that "they" had put together some things for Nori: clothes, toys, a bicycle, dolls and stuffed animals. The Deaf Ministry at our church, led by Joy White, a woman with a heart of gold and energy to burn when it came to doing for others, had also "adopted" Nori into their hearts.

THE ARKANSAS SCHOOL FOR THE DEAF

"For I know the plans I have for you,' declares the Lord, 'plans to prosper you and not to harm you, plans to give you hope and a future.'" —Jeremiah 29:11

Nori's 8th birthday in Little Rock

The next day school began for Nori. My wife had made arrangements with the school's principal, Mike Phillips, that Nori would have two teachers: one deaf and one hearing. Her first teachers were Christine Fahrenbach and Linda Johnson. Christine was an exceptional teacher who was deaf and Linda was one of my former students and an outstanding teacher as well. Nori was in good hands. Both teachers were proficient in the use of Sign Language, the deaf teacher especially in American Sign Language, a language in and of itself and different grammatically from English. Nori flourished. She was so excited about school that she would get up early, before Pat and me, and dress then go back to bed and lay awake until we got up. Her teachers and the other students loved her because of her enthusiasm and because she was a leader. She would be the first to try something and the first to get her classmates organized. At times she was too "pushy", too much the leader.

In my position at the University, I had occasion when I would go to the school to check on my students who were doing field work there. I always looked forward to those days because it gave me a chance to see

Nori. One day as I was walking down the hall to Mike's office, I passed Nori's classroom. She saw me and jumped out of her seat and ran to me and jumped into my arms and gave me a big hug. My heart melted. Her teacher, Susan Wright, "looked the other way". She had melted Susan's heart too. At home I would teasingly call her "my pest". She learned to fingerspell "pest". One day at school she told Susan that her dad called her "pest" which Nori took to mean as a complimentary word. Susan knew my personality, but she gave me a hard time about that anyway.

School was a wonderful time for Nori as she was involved in everything. I was so happy that she was athletic and she participated in all of the sports and extra-curricular activities including Singing Fingers. Singing Fingers was a group formed by Stacey Tatera, a former university student of mine. The little kids learned to sign songs and then they would travel to different places, Rotary for example or a special luncheon, and sign songs. They dressed in costume and they won over a lot of people. I really believe that people who knew little to nothing about the Deaf, came to love them all because of the deaf children they met in Singing Fingers. One day Stacey told me that they were going to perform in the student union at the University. My friend and colleague at the University, Dr. Jesse Dancer, and I were there for lunch and what a great performance they put on for the students and faculty. I wanted to get up and declare, "that's my daughter", but Nori would have been terribly embarrassed. Jesse I think felt the same way. We both just watched… and cheered. She was "growing up".

One small but at the time significant matter arose. The Little Rock School District informed me that Nori might have to attend public school as we lived in Little Rock and ASD was a state residential school, intended primarily for deaf students from around the state who had no or very limited access to appropriate education in their home district. Because Nori was not a US citizen, we also had to pay the district $5000 in tuition. Pat and I met with the District Associate Superintendent and pled our case for Nori's enrollment at ASD. And of course we wrote a check for $5000 to the School District. A few days later the Associate Superintendent called me back to his office. He informed me that the District, after conferring with ASD, was agreeable to Nori attending ASD. Then he reached in his desk drawer and pulled out an envelope. "Mr. Rittenhouse, the District requires me to receive a check from you for $5000, but noone said I have to cash it" and he handed me back the $5000. There were other people like this gentleman who God used to make Nori's new home in Little Rock special.

NORI'S FIRST DOCTOR'S VISIT

That first week of school, we took Nori to her new doctor for the first time. It was quite an experience for her as her very limited health care had been provided by missionaries in makeshift clinics in Tegucigalpa. Now she was in a clinic with an elevator, drinking fountains, comfortable chairs and even television. Her doctor gave her a thorough check-up and declared her healthy with a few problems that anti-biotics would take care of. When it was time for her first shot, the doctor told Nori that it would sting. Pat gestured to her that the needle would sting but that she would be fine. Pat communicated this information using mostly facial expressions and body language. Nori bravely stuck out her shoulder and acted like it was no big deal. However it did sting and she reacted. When the doctor was ready to give her the second shot, she didn't want it and Pat had to hold her and comfort her. Watching a seven-year-old child experience all these firsts, especially when you knew Nori's background, was to us like watching little miracles. Some even a little painful.

At that time in Nori's life we didn't think too much about the distant future if at all: dating, driving, college, work, marriage. Our energies were focused on her immigration situation, adoption efforts and giving her all the good and positive experiences we could….and fortunately we had plenty of good help. What a great place for a deaf child to get a start in life, Little Rock, Arkansas with our church, Fellowship Bible, and the School for the Deaf. From top to "bottom", the ASD teachers, administrators and staff were the best. The Superintendent was Susan Pack and did she love children. The first time I met Susan, she was giving a little child a haircut in her office. She had a smile that made your day and her personality permeated the entire campus. The Associate Superintendent who made it possible for Nori to attend ASD and many, many others lent a hand to a little girl from another part of the world so that she could have a better life. What a country we live in.

KROGERS

Often in life, on reflection, it's the little things that capture our hearts, that we remember best and with affection. I'll never forget Nori's first trip to Krogers. One Saturday morning (it was probably about a week after she had arrived) we made a trip to Krogers. Right away she was amazed that the door opened by itself. As best I could I explained how. I then grabbed a cart and put her in it. Up and down the aisles we went. Her eyes were as big as saucers as she took in all the colors, sizes, shapes, smells. It was like a Disneyland of food. Nori knew three or four Spanish words. One was "esta" and she would point at the various products and say "esta" meaning (I think) "what's the sign for that". I was a regular at Krogers and the workers there knew me. They got a real kick out of Nori's excitement. Our first trip to Krogers lasted nearly two hours, as I would give her the sign for banana, apple, milk, meat, etc. I would make the sign and she would in turn make it back to me. When first learning how to make signs, people often reverse the hand shape or the motion and sometimes the direction. But with Nori she almost always made the sign correctly the first time she tried it. To me it was an indication of her brightness, her aptitude for language and her hunger to communicate. Kroger for Nori in those early days was better than a trip to the zoo. She would always share her new vocabulary with her mom. The two of them very quickly bonded, especially I think when Nori fully realized that Pat couldn't hear either.

We got hearing aids for Nori and she wore them without putting up a fuss. Today as I write this book, Nori is 23 years old and she still wears them. Commonly the Deaf will stop wearing their hearing aids when they reach their teen years. That is due in part to modesty, in part to their full embracing of their deafness and their love of "their language", American Sign Language. While the medical community and society at large may see deafness as a disability, the Deaf do not view it in the same way. For them, their deafness and their language identify them not as disabled but as members of a minority group, a unique culture. Nori is no different but she still loves her hearing aids, very likely now because she loves to listen to music.

Nori following her first year in Little Rock

My wife Pat is a language arts teacher, a master teacher as any of her principals, teaching colleagues and students will tell you. She is exceptional. It seemed that everything we did at home (meals, prayers, games, etc) she turned into a language-learning lesson. One of the most unique things was bathtub language learning. Nori loved to take baths…and we loved for her to take baths. Pat would fill up the tub with nice warm water and then while Nori was in the tub, we could get a little break from the very demanding Nori (the "pest"). Pat put a big plastic pocket chart on the tiled wall and each night she would put ten pictures of objects (animals, food, transportation items, etc) in the pockets and teach Nori the signs. Then Nori would have to practice the signs. She also had magic markers in the tub and Nori would practice writing words and simple sentences on the tiles. Often while doing these activities Nori would "sing". We would sit in the living room in our small house and laugh sometimes almost to tears at Nori "singing" the words. Pat says her own creativity has blossomed because of her principal at ASD, Theda Gatlin, who Pat says allowed her to try new things without the usual "red tape". Theda was another administrator who put students first... always.

NORI'S NEW HOME

Outwardly Nori made a quick adjustment to her new home. However, at first we were not so sure that the inward adjustment had been made. She saved EVERYTHING: gum wrappers, wrapping paper, shopping bags, price tags....EVERYTHING. When Pat was straightening up Nori's drawers she came across this large cache of "nothing". She sat down with Nori and explained that she could throw a lot of the stuff away. But Nori insisted on keeping everything. It turned out that Nori expected to be sent back to Honduras and she wanted to take everything back with her, not knowing what her Honduran friends might want. Gently Pat explained to Nori that she was not going back to Honduras except to visit, that she now had a permanent home and a permanent family. Nori was pleased and happy to hear this news...but she continued to save "stuff".

May my prayer be set before You. May the lifting up of my hands be like the evening sacrifice. Psalm 141:2

At night before bedtime, we would pray with Nori. I would first say/sign a prayer asking for protection and help for Nori. Pat would then say a short prayer usually asking the Lord for something very specific for Nori such as "please help Nori to share" (Nori did not like to share her things). Then it was Nori's turn. She would relive her day at ASD and thank God ("I thank you God, story about little boy, thank you God" and on and on and on). At first her prayers were fairly short and gestural but as she began to increase her sign vocabulary and develop more sophisticated language, her prayers got longer and longer and longer. I have a bad lower back from an old football injury and it would begin to ache. But "my ego" would not allow me to sit down. As an "older" dad, I didn't want Nori to think "my dad is old" so I would stand throughout her prayer. Many times Pat would sign to her "Amen" and Nori would end her prayer. The next morning when Pat would turn on the hall light signaling it was time to get ready for school, Nori would climb out of her bunk bed already dressed and ready to go. She had gotten up sometime during the night and dressed for school. She absolutely loved her school, her teachers and her classmates. Nori had gone from an abandoned child, an orphan, to a daughter, sister, granddaughter, student all in lightning speed and she adjusted to the transition as if "of course, this is where I'm supposed to be". God truly was at work in this little girl's life. His Goodness was everywhere, always.

Nori's "learning bathtub"

Your hands made me and formed me; teach me to understand your commands. Psalm 119:73

Our church, Fellowship Bible, was a wonderful church. While we attended service, which was interpreted so beautifully for the Deaf by Barbara and a lady named Mindy Hooper, the children attended classes. Nori and Noel loved their classes and both participated without an interpreter, a "total immersion" experience. This was our wish, as we wanted Nori to develop mainstream skills, "real-life" skills. She did so well and got along great with the hearing kids. We give a lot of credit (and thanks) to her Sunday School teachers.

NORI'S FIRST CHRISTMAS

No eye has seen, no ear has heard and no mind has imagined what God has prepared for those who love Him. 1 Corinthians 2:9

Most all of our family members were in Illinois (Bloomington and the Chicago area). Our first Christmas with Nori was a time of excitement for her...and for us. We had put up a tree at home in Little Rock, she'd had a Christmas party at school and she knew that she would met her new sisters, Julie and Nancy, and Grandmas in Illinois. As best we could we told her what Christmas meant. We told her the story of the birth of Jesus, who He was, and what He promised. That is a challenge for anyone to explain to a seven year old, but even more challenging to a little girl like Nori. But Nori seemed to accept the story as if "what's the big deal". We packed the car with all the presents and on Saturday after Pat's last day of teaching before the holidays, we all packed into the car including our (now Nori's) dogs Dusty and Duffy and got onto I-40 headed north. Nori had a million questions and in the short time between August and now December, her communication skills had really improved along with her comprehension. Each time she had a question she would say "Dad" and I'd tap Pat (who remember couldn't hear) and Pat would answer her question. Much of the conversation was about her new family and presents. Pat however worked in the Jesus story and told Nori that Christmas was like a birthday party, Jesus' birthday. And Nori said with eyes as big as silver dollars "will Jesus be there?". Pat thought for a minute and then said "Yes Jesus will be there". It was the perfect question and only Nori in her youth and innocence could have asked it. It is a question that led us to read the Jesus story to the family on Christmas Eve and emphasize Jesus' presence even though we couldn't see Him, at least with our eyes.

Nori's first Christmas in Illinois

At future Christmas gatherings, when my grand daughter Hailey was a little older, Hailey would read the story from Matthew and Nori would sign along with her. Both girls would also sing Christmas carols together, Hailey in voice and Nori in Sign. They loved to entertain, especially Nori. She felt that first Christmas, I think for maybe the first time, a real sense of belonging. She wanted to know who everyone was and especially how she and they were related. Nori was so excited to meet her family and to know who was who. She loved Julie and Nancy her new sisters, my daughters from my first marriage. She also became very close to her two Grammas, particularly my mom. My mom was only 4'10" tall and I think Nori was "impressed" with her size. She called Mom Little Gramma and Pat's mom Big Gramma. It was a great Christmas and Nori fit right in. She liked to say "my sister Julie, my sister Nancy".

Soon after we returned from Nori's first Christmas with her new family, a deaf visitor came to our house for dinner. His name was Ron Sipek and he was a vocational rehabilitation counselor. There was a national convention in town and he was attending. Ron's parents were deaf and he was a highly skilled user of American Sign Language. He and Nori talked for a long time that night. Ron was clearly impressed with Nori's rapidly developing ASL skills. He found it hard to believe that Nori had only been in an ASL environment for four months. At the same time that Nori's ASL skills were developing, her reading skills and vocabulary were coming along slowly at best. Her late start in school and her hunger to communicate in her native language, American Sign Language, were working against her progress in the acquisition of English. While we were thrilled that Nori's world was opening up through her ability to now communicate, we were concerned with her slow reading and writing progress. Today, 16 years later, Nori is a junior at Gallaudet University in Washington, DC and her English language ability has improved greatly as attested to by her 3.0+ GPA.

DISNEYWORLD

Nori at DisneyWorld in Orlando

We decided that during spring break we would take Nori to Disneyworld. We ordered a tape from them and began to introduce her to Mickey, Minnie, Donald Duck and all of the wonderful Disney characters. She told her friends at school and her teachers about her upcoming trip and they told her how exciting it would be. As the time to head south drew near, we were as excited as everyone else about Nori's excitement and how she'd react. For her, Krogers had seemed like Disneyland; what would she be like in Orlando? We packed and left early that Saturday morning. We drove the whole way the same day.

Nori loved to talk and to ask questions. She sat in the back seat and we tied a jump rope to Pat's armrest and gave the other end to Nori. Whenever Nori wanted to talk to her mom, she would just pull on the jump rope. This way we eliminated the middleman….me the driver.

Before arriving to Disneyworld, we stopped at a Florida rest stop. It was a neat rest area because they had some equipment for kids to play on and the equipment was fashioned after Disney characters. Nori jumped out of the car and ran to "Mickey" and hopped on. She ran from character to character, all excited that she had arrived at Disneyworld and it was all she had envisioned and more. We could hardly contain ourselves. When we had to break the news to Nori that this was just a rest stop and we would be leaving soon she was confused. Pat as only Pat can explained it all to her and we hopped back in our car. Disneyworld did turn out to be all Nori had hoped for and we enjoyed it, as we never had before. It took both of us to watch her, as she would run from one Disney thing to another. The further into each day we got, the more energized she would be. It took both of us to keep up with her.

A few years later we returned to Florida so that Nori could meet her Honduran family, her biological mother, and her sisters. It was a moving and very emotional meeting and we spent two days together. We rented rooms at a nice motel for the family that had brought Nori into the world and raised her for seven years and the kids swam most of the time. It was important for Nori's well being that she have a total sense of self. She and her cousins, sisters and mom got along great and they were clearly touched by Nori's progress and good fortune. She visits them now at least once a year.

Nori in Singing Fingers performing at UALR

After returning from spring break Nori got involved in Singing Fingers, the sign group made up of the younger children at ASD that I mentioned earlier. Nori loved performing almost from Day One, but Singing Fingers brought out the "theater" that would become one of her many talents. She loved getting into costume, learning the songs and being a special part of "her new family". Stacey and her team treated the kids as if they were their own children and Nori and her Singing Fingers friends could do no wrong in Stacey's eyes. I believe with all my heart that Nori's experience with Singing Fingers helped give her confidence and her fearlessness that has carried her so far. God in His own way had begun to put the people in Nori's life who would help her become all that He intended for her.

LEARNING TO RIDE A BICYCLE

Nori was very natural at sports and participated in everything while in school. She began her sports career at the Arkansas School for the Deaf, playing basketball, volleyball and swimming. It was also in Little Rock that first full summer that she learned to ride a bicycle. When our church friends discovered that Nori had come to Little Rock with only a very small suitcase of belongings (that didn't even include a pair of pajamas) they quickly took care of that problem. She was brought dresses, shoes, pants and tops, you name it. And a bicycle!

Nori being taught to ride her bike by our neighbor

I taught her how to ride her bike in front of our Little Rock home. She would start at the neighbor's house and try to ride to our house. When she'd fall (which was every time she tried at first), I'd sign to her "improvement". Improve or improvement is signed by putting one hand at the wrist of the other arm and with a very light movement advance it up the arm. Little improvement would be a slight movement and big improvement was a big movement. As soon as she fell, she'd look up to see how she'd done. I made sure to always show some improvement but also to let her know she still had a ways to go. She never cried even when she took some hard falls. A little encouragement went a long way with Nori. And boy could you see her competitive spirit shine through. I'll never forget the day she made it all the way. As she passed me on the sidewalk, I signed "IMPROVEMENT" by going all the way from the wrist to the top of the shoulder. She was smiling that big Nori smile and kept right on going. She only knew one way to stop at that point and that's what she did: she just turned her bike over and fell off….still smiling. By the end of the summer, with a few scrapes and bruises to show for her efforts, she was riding with no hands and her feet up on the handlebars…and smiling that Nori smile that everyone knows who knows Nori. A year had passed and Pat and I had come to realize that God really has great plans for all of us, Americans, Hondurans, Black, White, rich, poor and His Hand of Favor is on us all. Surely it was on Nori.

CAR ACCIDENT

One evening while I was interpreting for David and Jean King at their home, I received a call from the hospital: Nori and her mom had been in a car accident. I rushed to the hospital praying all the way. When I arrived, Nori was sitting up in bed with a big bandage wrapped around her head….and a big smile on her face. She and her mom had been driving home and signing to each other. At a stop light , Pat rear-ended the car in front of her. Neither had her seat belt on. Pat was not hurt and Nori, while hurt, couldn't wait to get back to school to show off her wrappings and the hospital bracelet which she didn't take off for several days. It was a frightening but valuable lesson for both of them but especially Nori. She now drives her own car and never departs until everyone has their seatbelts on.

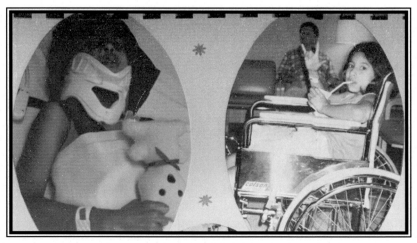

Nori following the car accident

36

Nori the ballplayer

SPORTS AND RECREATION

During the next school year, Nori played basketball for the elementary Girls team and was a cheerleader for the Boys. She earned her place on both squads with her ability but more so with her enthusiasm. She loved to be around the ball and even though she was a guard (a "bush" was what one of her coaches called her) she loved to go inside (where the "trees" were, the same coach said). When she'd get the ball inside, because she was so small, she'd cover up the ball and hold it tightly in her arms. Her coach gave her the nickname "Squirrel" because she looked like a squirrel protecting a nut. That nickname has stuck and she uses it as her email name today. And there watching her and encouraging her was Houston Nutt. It meant so much to me that Houston would take time out of his busy schedule to support Nori. His sons were all Division I coaches, his grand children were all top athletes and he served as Chairman of the Board of Directors of the Arkansas School for the Deaf. But he "made the time".

Nori learned to swim that year as well. She would first cry when she'd get in the water but her coach Trina was very patient with her always saying, "You can do it Nori". And just as with the bicycle, she persevered and became a very good swimmer. Ironically (or was it), Trina's dad was the former swimming coach at the University where I worked and Trina was not only an accomplished swimmer, but also a natural teacher. Once again, God's Goodness was evident to us.

SUMMER CAMPS

Nori at the summer leadership camp in South Dakota

We also enrolled Nori in summer camps every year. She attended camps for the Deaf all over the United States. She made a number of friends and re-connected with many of them in college. Her favorite camp was a sports camp in Louisville, Kentucky (the Mini Deaf Olympics). She attended that camp every summer for three summers and even recruited some friends to attend with her. We enjoyed taking her to camps as we would vacation in the area until the camp was over. She also attended the Aspen Camp for the Deaf, the Leadership Camp in South Dakota, the Math and Science Camp in Arizona, the Space Camp in Huntsville, Alabama and several church camps. Nori is out-going and fearless and we think her camp experiences gave her, in part, this self-confidence.

NORI'S PERSPECTIVE

At the age of 13, about five years after leaving Honduras, Nori wrote about her experiences in her new home which we published (it follows). While the perspective is Nori's, her mom helped her with the grammar and some of the word choices.

Nori as a HomeComing Attendant at the Arkansas School for the Deaf

MY NEW LIFE by Nori Oyuki
dedicated to my family

I was born in Tegucigalpa, Honduras. I don't remember much about growing up in Honduras but I remember a little bit about what Honduras looks like. Honduras looks very poor. Most roads are made of dirt. Many homes look like they will fall apart. Stray dogs, cats, roosters, chickens were everywhere. There were many beggars, both children and adults. Some people sold food on sticks. Honduras is very different from the U.S.

In February 1996, Pat Rittenhouse and her friends went to Honduras to help poor people. They helped doctors give medicine, etc. A Honduran woman saw me with no parents, no school in her neighborhood. Then the woman went to see Carlos and talked about me.

Later Pat Rittenhouse asked Carlos, "Are there any deaf orphans?" Carlos said "Which, boys or girls?" Pat said it didn't matter. Then he said, "Yes there is one deaf girl. I will meet you tomorrow and will try to get Nori". Pat Rittenhouse said okay but in two days her friends had to go back to Arkansas. That morning Pat got ready to leave but happen Carlos and I came to meet Pat. She was surprised to see Carlos and me. Pat met me, then she taught me to spell in sign language my name. I didn't know how to use sign language. Then Pat had to leave to go back to Arkansas. I stayed in Honduras. Pat arrived in Arkansas then later she told Bob her husband about me.

Pat and Bob went back to Honduras to visit me in June. Pat and Bob met me, then Bob and I played a game. Bob was all the time losing and I all the time won but I made up rules to play game. Bob and Pat said bye to me, then they went back to Arkansas. Two months later I planned to fly on an airplane to Arkansas.

On August 6, 1996, I was age seven (almost eight) alone on airplane arrived at Houston, Texas. Then Pat and I arrived to the Little Rock airport. I saw many of Pat's friends. I was too shy and didn't know who were her friends. I saw Bob and ran to hug him. I knew Pat and Bob, that was all. Pat's friends Jean and her husband and her daughter Noel met me. Noel hugged me but I was too shy.

I didn't know how to use sign language, play different games, abc, count numbers and many other things. Later I went to school for the first time. I was in Pat's room at the high school. I waited for Bob to get me to register. Then I met too many people. Later I packed my backpack with things to get ready for school the next day. I slept, then in the morning I woke up at about 4 AM. I shhh kept quiet and put on my clothes, then went back to sleep. Later Pat shook me awake then saw I was already ready for school. Pat was surprised I was too excited to go to school.

School started at 8 AM. I had two teachers. The deaf teacher used sign language and no voice. She taught me in the morning. The other teacher used signs and talked. She taught me in the afternoon. I entered class but I didn't know how to use sign language. The teacher tried hard to use sign language with me but also used hand gestures to make me understand. When school finished then we went home. I didn't know how to ride a bike but Bob taught me how to ride a bike then I fell and laughed. I tried to practice biking but it was too hard for me.

Then Pat forced me to go to bath about one hour but I enjoyed my bath. My voice sing very loud then Bob sick of me because I sing too loud. Then I went to bed quiet read but Pat taught me the calendar. I still learn lots. Next day I enjoyed school. We went swimming at school. I stepped down to touch the water then I cried because I was afraid of deep water. Then the swimming teacher Becky taught me how to swim. Finish swimming then we went home.

I cooked. I made tortillas, eggs, and beans. I enjoyed cooking. That was the only thing I knew how to cook. Three years later I knew sign language very well. I was so happy to learn sign language, play different games, abc, count numbers, swimming and biking.

Later when I was eight years old I called Pat "Mom" and Bob "Dad". In the middle of July 1999, my mom and I moved to Arizona because my m told me about a good school and many Mexican people. My dad had to stay in Arkansas because he had to finish work. Then August 5, 1999 I was with Kyara, my babysitter, and met people but I was too shy and I didn't know who was Kyara's friends. Later I became used to the new school and friends.

How do I feel about Honduras, Arkansas and Arizona? I miss Honduras, but I am so lucky I moved to the U.S. I learned lots of things but I still love my first country. In Arkansas, I was seven years old and in school there I learned lots of new things. I enjoyed learning sign language. In Arizona, WOW! Many opportunities in Arizona. I go to summer school, play volleyball, basketball, swim team, more sports, went to Space Camp in Alabama and climbed Mount Lemmon and went kayaking. I have many deaf friends near my house. **THE END**

THE LATER SCHOOL YEARS

Do not conform any longer to the pattern of this world, but be transformed by the renewing of your mind. Then you will be able to test and approve what God's will is-His good, pleasing and perfect will. Romans 12:2

THE ARIZONA SCHOOL FOR THE DEAF

Nori and her cousin Elizabeth from New Hampshire

In 1999, Nori and Pat moved to Tucson Arizona. When Nori's immigration status as an exchange student expired after three months with us, we ignored it. For almost three years we lived in fear that she might have to go back to Honduras. Of course, she was unaware of "the politics" of her situation. We had applied for adoption but the process ground slowly. Our Judge had a reputation as being philosophically against inter-racial adoptions and she considered Nori's adoption to fall into that category. We had presented official papers from Honduras stipulating that she had been abandoned and we had presented a supported argument that as a deaf child, Nori was going to be in a home where both mother and father could communicate with her. We emphasized that Pat was deaf and was a teacher of the Deaf. Our arguments did us little good with this Judge. After three years, Nori's eligibility to attend the Arkansas School for the Deaf ran out and we were left with few options. One was to home school her and there was a mother in our church who home-schooled a few children. She also signed but we felt that Nori had done so well at ASD that we needed to pursue a more traditional educational setting for her.

I began my university work at Illinois State University back in 1977 as an Assistant Professor and Head of the Deaf Education Program. My colleague was Pat McAnally and Pat, now Dr. Pat McAnally, was the Assistant Superintendent of the Arizona School for the Deaf in Tucson. Because the school was close to the Mexican border I reasoned that the State of Arizona might be in a position to accommodate us. I called Pat McAnally and told her about our dilemma. Pat checked Arizona state rules and even though Nori was not an American Citizen, she could still attend the Tucson School. "Come on down" she said. It was late April. For us in our professional fields, it was very late to be making such a move. We decided to go for it anyway in hopes that Pat could get a job there. I was to remain at the University for one year and be sure that an orderly transition could occur. At that point, I had won two, large federal grants and was Director of the Program and did not feel at all comfortable leaving on such short notice so close to the beginning of the summer and fall terms. Pat applied for a teaching position right away and was hired. I traveled to Tucson on occasion and we would exchange emails during that year of transition. Nori adjusted beautifully and with the large Mexican student body at ASDB, she felt she was back in Honduras…with all the luxuries of living in the United States. The year went well for her and in addition to doing well at school she joined the basketball, track and softball teams.

Soon after Pat and Nori's arrival in Tucson, we were able to have our adoption petition heard by a new judge. He, on his first day after receiving our petition, approved the adoption. Nori and Pat flew back to Little Rock for "Nori's day in court" and a big celebration followed. Many of Nori's deaf friends from the Arkansas School for the Deaf, her former teachers and her old friends from Fellowship Bible Church attended the adoption event in court that day.

The Campus Superintendent of the Arizona School for the Deaf decided to retire that year and I was encouraged to apply for the position. In March I was named Campus Superintendent and in June of 2000, I joined Pat and Nori in Tucson. By now Nori was communicating as well as the native signers, had gotten involved in theater and was a leader on the campus. She was growing and adapting and I would joke that she was now a "fully spoiled American" just like her friends. Nori did well at the Tucson School and excelled in sports and in school.

HIGH SCHOOL

However, in 2002 we decided to uproot and move to Knoxville, Tennessee. 911 had happened the year before, we felt somewhat isolated from our families back in the middle of the country and so we began applying for positions in Knoxville. We chose Knoxville because I had won a sabbatical for the 1994-95 academic year and we had spent two weeks there collecting data for my sabbatical project. Pat took the year off and we traveled across the United States as part of the Project. We fell in love with Knoxville; mild winters, beautiful mountains and it seemed close to everything. The next year Nori came to be with us, and Knoxville became just a good memory. With God opening doors, Pat was offered a teaching position at the Tennessee School for the Deaf and I was offered the position of Executive Director of the Knoxville Center of the Deaf. We moved. Nori adapted quickly. Once again Nori excelled in school. One of her achievements was to win the Patsy Smith Sportsman's trophy as the school's outstanding athlete her first year at the school. While we felt that the Tennessee School for the Deaf was a fine school, we elected to enroll Nori at the large public High School, West High School, near our home the second year. While a student at West, Nori was highlighted in a special story in the newspaper, the Knoxville News Sentinel, for her academic excellence. She also was a member of the West High Girls basketball team, although she was not a starter as she had been previously at TSD.

NORI LEARNS TO DRIVE

Nori learned to drive while in high school. One thing that surprised and impressed us was that Nori didn't push us to drive. For her, driving at sixteen was not a given. It was the summer before her junior year that Pat and I decided that we needed to begin laying out a plan for teaching her to drive. Nori is barely five feet tall and she is petite. Couple that with any dad's nervousness about his teenage daughter driving independently and you can see why I lost a few nights' sleep over this important next phase in Nori's life. We first contracted with a driving school so that she could have some practice behind the wheel in a controlled environment. Then I began to take her to a large grocery store parking lot that was now vacant as the store had moved and we practiced parking and a few "moves". Nori did well, but street driving still put me in a funk. Finally Pat took the reins and she and Nori began driving on the street in traffic. As I'd watch them pull away, I'd think to myself "Nori's head barely sticks above the steering wheel". I'll have to admit I was surprised at how well she did. She picked up driving almost like she picked up everything else: "what's the big deal". She took her car (her mom's hand me down) to college and has it with her today at Gallaudet. She drives all over including to Rochester to visit old friends at NTID, Chicago where she has many friends and of course back and forth to Knoxville. She's never had an accident although she did once hit a deer…. while driving a rental car.

NORI DELIVERS WEST HIGH SCHOOL'S COMMENCEMENT ADDRESS

I can do everything through Him who gives me strength. Phillipians 4:13

Nori graduated in May 2007 and was selected to deliver the commencement address. West is a 1500 student High School with a stellar reputation. One of their traditions is to select three students to deliver commencement addresses. Nori was one of the students selected. The title of her presentation was "The Wind Beneath My Wings" and the audience was moved, many to tears. Here is her commencement address:

"People who face obstacles in our world sometimes feel lost and give up. They feel obstacles are impossible overcome and they lose hope. Many people feel like they will not succeed in the future. They cannot do anything about it. But some have someone who is their inspiration. They look at that person to remind them, they can do to succeed; they have hope; and their obstacles can be overcome.

I am one of those people. When I was seven years old, I started school for the first time. I did not know how to read, write, or count. My education was delayed compared to everyone else. I struggled and suffered that I had to catch up in school. I thought that I could not catch up and the students would move on to a higher level in school without me. It was slow process for me to learn and improve. Many times I wanted give up. It seems impossible. I would work so hard on my English everyday. I would be so tired of it, but I had to keep working on it. What Newt Gingrich said is so true: "Perseverance is the hard work you do after you get tired of doing the hard work you already did." I decided to accept struggle when I thought of one person who was succeed. I knew my struggle was not impossible.

Shirley Venis is my inspiration. She and I were both born in Honduras. We are both deaf and we struggled with reading and writing language. She wanted become a teacher. In Honduras, many people do not believe that the Deaf can become teachers. Shirley asked to be enrolled in a teacher preparation school, but they denied her. She kept trying to enroll, over and over and over. Finally, they let her enroll to study become a teacher of Deaf. After three years, she became a teacher. Sometimes the attitudes of the people are obstacles. Another obstacle was that Shirley struggled with the Spanish language because she was deaf. She was stubborn however, and she did not give up. She showed me that I can do it just like her.

I realize that many people have obstacles in their lives. One of my heroes, Michael Jordan said "Obstacles don't have to stop you. If you run into a wall, don't turn around and give up. Figure out how to climb it, go through it, or work around it." Shirley did figure out how to climb over her wall. I must do the same. Obstacles are often not easy to overcome. We have to face obstacles and figure out how to find other way around them. I may be frustrated at times, but I must fight on and not give up in a world full of obstacles.

So, Class of 2007, we all will face some sort of obstacles in our life, whether it be a disability, the color of your skin, your education, your family, your background, your whatever…, you must decide that you will overcome that obstacle. Make your obstacle your footstool so that you can soar to greater heights".

Nori Oyuki Barahona Burgos Rittenhouse
West High School Commencement Address
Knoxville, Tennessee
June 2007

She signed her presentation in American Sign Language and her interpreter while a student at West, Ruby Warner, voiced for her. Nori stressed the independence and strength of deaf people and concluded by saying that obstacles in life are merely footstools for opportunity. Here is what the local paper had to say about Nori the next day:

DEAF STUDENT LEAVES HER IMPRINT ON WEST GRADS

Nori Rittenhouse is one of those people to whom you can't help but pay attention. She has perfect Pantene curls, a welcoming smile and shows no timidity in hugging a stranger. Oh, and she is deaf. But that last detail is just a formality if you asked her. Rittenhouse has never let that minor inconvenience get in her way.

On Saturday, Rittenhouse gave a senior speech during graduation ceremonies for West High School at the Knoxville Civic Coliseum-a first for the high school and possibly for Knox County Schools.

But it was not an honor given to Rittenhouse because of her disability. She tried out for the slot just as dozens of seniors did, submitting an essay in English class and then presenting it before judges who chose the top three. Rittenhouse would never accept a handout, and those who know her would say she doesn't need one anyway.

Teacher Patsy Lowe is not surprised that Rittenhouse would take on such a task. Rittenhouse signed the speech while lead interpreter Ruby Warner voiced the words. "She is outgoing, enthusiastic and she tries anything new. She is a very brave person," Lowe said. "She does not limit herself in any way."

Rittenhouse chose to attend a "hearing school" instead of the Tennessee School for the Deaf because she wanted the challenge. After all, it has been the challenges she faced in life that made her stronger.

Rittenhouse was born in Honduras, adopted by an American family and started school for the first time in the United States at age seven. She was illiterate. Her speech Saturday was about overcoming challenges. At first she thought students at West would underestimate or ignore her, but that fear only motivated her to work harder, she said.

Rittenhouse played basketball and ran track, was in advanced drama, studied Spanish and mentored freshmen, both hearing and deaf. "Deaf people can work hard," Rittenhouse said. "We're not weak. We're strong."

And in many ways, Rittenhouse is like any other graduating senior. She's excited for the freedom of college-she will attend The National Technical Institute for the Deaf in Rochester, NY,-considering a career in photography and acting, and nervous about standing before the entire student body.

By the end of her speech Saturday, it was obvious she has left an impression on her fellow graduates in her time at West. Instead of clapping for her, they raised their hands, fingers spread wide, and they waved them-an ovation in sign language. "Sometimes people's attitudes are our obstacles," Rittenhouse said. "But they don't have to stop you. We have to make those obstacles our footstools.

The Knoxville News Sentinel
June 4, 2007

Our once little girl, now an 18 year old young woman, from Tegucigalpa, Honduras had come a very long way.

NORI RETURNS TO TEGUCIGALPA

Therefore go and make disciples of all nations, baptizing them in the name of the Father and of the Son and of the Holy Spirit. Matthew 28:19

Upon Nori's graduation from West High, in the summer before she started her college experience at the National Technical Institute for the Deaf in Rochester, New York, she traveled back to Tegucigalpa, her homeland, on a mission trip. It was a wonderful "homecoming". Some of the kids from the orphanage and her neighborhood remembered her, then seven years old, now 18. It was moving for Nori as well. She spent two weeks there volunteering everyday in the classrooms of the Happy Hands Christian School for the Deaf. The little girl who couldn't write, fingerspell or say her name 11 years earlier, was now teaching other deaf children before heading off to college. She had come full circle: the beautiful child adopted by missionaries was now on a mission trip back to the very place she had left for a new beginning. She was now an emissary for God. His Hand of Favor was upon her. His Goodness was upon us.

Nori delivering the commencement address at West High School

HAPPY HANDS CHRISTIAN SCHOOL FOR THE DEAF

Happy Hands Christian School for the Deaf in Tegucigalpa

It sorrowed us and it sorrowed Nori to think of all the deaf children of Honduras who held God's promise too, but may never have the opportunity to realize it. Nori's visit touched her deeply. Over the years, Pat has worked hard to support the new Happy Hands School for the Deaf in Tegucigalpa, Honduras, known as Manos Felices. Manos Felices is part of the New Life Deaf Ministry of Tegucigalpa and NLDM's Executive Director is Christy Owen, a remarkable woman. Christy is from Texas and Little Rock and has been there for 13 years. She had gone there as a missionary while she was working at the University of Arkansas at Little Rock where I also worked. Christy decided to step out in faith and move to Tegucigalpa for a two-year missionary stint in 1999. Two years stretched to 13 and today Christy is still going strong. She will tell you it is by the Grace of God. She has adopted a Honduran child, Lillian who has severe disabilities and who is now a young woman. Christy's heart is with the Deaf Hondurans and that love can be seen in the wonderful New Life Deaf Ministry. Recently I was returning from Honduras and bumped into a Honduran lady at the airport who was from Tegucigalpa. She had married an American man and was headed home to Atlanta. We struck up a conversation and I told her about Nori and how desperate families were for some kind of education for their deaf children back in 1996. I said "there was just nothing in the way of education for Nori" and before I could finish my sentence she said "and now it's so wonderful here for deaf children" and she threw up her hands in celebration.

Manos Felices is led by a Honduran educator Oneida Aguilar who is married to Efrain, a deaf man who is himself also very accomplished. Through Christy's efforts and the day to day active and supportive leadership of Oneida, the deaf children and their parents now have great hope for the future. If anyone reading this book has a heart for the Deaf and is looking for an exemplary mission to support I highly recommend New Life Deaf Ministry. You can contribute by writing to New Life Deaf Ministry of Honduras, P.O.Box 55184, Little Rock, AR 72215-5184or check out their website at www.nldm.org. NLDM is a 501C-3 tax-exempt organization and your donation is tax deductible. It will steal your heart.

Had Manos Felices been in existence when Nori was a young child, we might not have her today as our beloved daughter. We are so so thankful that it was God's Plan to make her ours. And we are grateful to God for the Hand of Favor that He has placed on Christy.

EPILOGUE

In his heart a man plans his course, but the Lord determines his footsteps. Proverbs 16:9

COLLEGE IN NEW YORK

With her high school degree in hand, Nori headed to college in the fall of 2007. Nori became a freshman in the National Technical Institute for the Deaf at the Rochester Institute of Technology. Nori had wanted to attend Gallaudet University, the only four-year university for the Deaf in the world. However there was turmoil on the campus and the school faced sanctions from the federal government over the quality of its program. So Nori choose NTID in Rochester, New York.

NORI THE ACTRESS

Nori as Gretel in the Interact play Hansel and Gretel

Nori was in the school play at NTID. Her director told us that she was a natural and needed very little coaching. We give a lot of credit to the experiences she had in her various camps where theater was always an activity, to Singing Fingers at ASD in Little Rock and to Interact, a theater group for the Deaf, in Knoxville founded by Carol LaCava and Kim Hinchey. Nori was in several of their plays including one starring role as Gretel in **Hansel and Gretel**. Interact is a wonderful theater group, one of the Knoxville Deaf Community's best-kept secrets. Nori even considers Kim her "big sister" and they get together whenever Nori is in town. She was in one play at Gallaudet but to my chagrin she has not continued with her theater work. Hopefully someday she will regain her enthusiasm for acting, as she is a natural as her NTID director declared.

While a student at NTID, God's Goodness was present in the people he surrounded her with: Laurie Mosely, her academic advisor, Mindy Hopper, at the time a doctoral student at the University of Rochester now Dr. Mindy Hopper and Marilyn Mitchell, an interpreter and instructor at NTID. Laurie and Mindy are both deaf and Marilyn has been around deafness practically her whole life. Laurie is one of those people who works extra hard for her students and would probably do so even if she was not paid. With all of the university, certification and other course requirements and the bureaucracy within the university, college life can get complicated. Laurie was always there for Nori, guiding, helping, nurturing and encouraging. Mindy was a former student of mine at Illinois State University, an exceptional student. She was one of the first deaf students in Illinois to be mainstreamed and an avowed oralist when she came to ISU. After graduating and becoming a deafness professional she went through a transformation and now argues persuasively and scholarly for the ASL position of communication. Marilyn and I go way back (to the 1960s) to my first teaching assignment at the then Minnesota School for the Deaf. She befriended my family and was so helpful to me as a young father. Marilyn took Nori under her wing and became her "Aunt" on the NTID campus. When Marilyn moved to California to be near her son and his family, Nori purchased her car.

GALLAUDET UNIVERSITY

In May of 2010, she graduated from NTID with an Associates Degree in Graphic Technology. Now she was off to Gallaudet where today she is a junior in the Family and Child Studies Program, hoping to graduate in May of 2013. Once again, when difficulties arose, good people stepped in: Dr. Robert Weinstock and Chrissy Medina. Robert stepped in when Nori was denied acceptance into a special program at Gallaudet, reviewed her application and background and admitted her. Chrissy served as her academic advisor her first critical year at Gallaudet and guided her through the first year of study. She was always available to Nori and took on an advocate's personality. We so appreciated her and now miss her. Nori chose Child and Family Studies because of an internship that she served at the Texas Lion's Camp the summer of 2009. The Texas Lions Camp is the largest Lions Camp in the United States. The Director, Paul Brouse, is the husband of Mindy Brouse, one of my former students and one of my wife Pat's student teachers. They are a wonderful couple with six children and Mindy home schools them all. Mindy was probably the most enthusiastic student I've ever taught and would have been a wonderful teacher but chose instead to raise her family. Nori loved her time at camp and decided to wed her technology with her new found love for working with children who have disabilities by majoring in Child and Family Studies at Gallaudet.

Nori playing ball for West High School

SPORTS AT GALLAUDET

Today, Nori is a member of the track team where she runs the 100, 200 and 4x100 relay. She's not the fastest nor the most productive athlete on the track team but this year (2012) she won The Most Improved Award, given for her hard work.

Nori carries a full load at Gallaudet and going into her senior year has earned a 3.0+ cumulative grade point average that she is determined to improve on. Recently (May 2012), she came home to attend the wedding of Sarah Beam, the daughter of Phil and Lynn Beam, a deaf couple in Knoxville. Phil is himself adopted and he and Nori have developed a close and special bond. They never fail to get together when Nori is home and the Beams, both devout Christians and members of our church, have been deaf adults who Nori looks up to and who have always encouraged her. Phil is probably the best "listener" one could ever hope to meet and he always finds a way to look for the good in everything. While she was home for the wedding, we talked about her Gallaudet plans and she went on and on about the heavy load she wanted to take. I tried to encourage her to balance her college life and to have fun along the way. A year ago, she would have kissed me and thanked me for seeing how important the party life in college is. But this time she said "Dad I've had my college fun; I'm an adult now and I must focus on my academic work." Praise Jesus!

Nori also works in the Gallaudet post office and just as she did with the West High School commencement address, she sought out the post office job on her own and won the position even though the job description indicated the position was not for first year students at Gallaudet. She loves the post office work, the extra spending money and keeping busy. She just recently passed her English Proficiency exam and is in the middle of an intense interim-period, three week psychology course in her major. We can't wait for her to come home for a few weeks this summer before she heads back to Gallaudet for the home stretch of her studies. In April of 2012, Nori went on a Gallaudet mission trip to Costa Rica. As you can see from her Gallaudet report, she praised the Deaf of Costa Rica as being strong and resilient and not "spoiled" as Americans can be.

MY TRIP TO COSTA RICA

a) What did you learn about Costa Ricans and their culture that had the most impact on you?

The Costa Rican people seemed to spend more time outdoors doing various activities such as socializing in their local parks, skating or skateboarding, and creating artwork in the streets. The Costa Ricans seemed to be more "approachable". They were easy to meet and connect with. They don't bury themselves in technology like people in America. Here in America people seem more isolated from each other because they are always busy listening to someone through their phones or music through their earphones. However, the Costa Ricans seem to be more people-oriented. The environment was different that way. Instead of seeing people hooked to their smart phones and iPods, etc., they were involved with each other face-to-face, playing sports and chatting.

Costa Rican food reminds me of the food in my home country of Honduras. There is a lot of beans and rice in their every day diet. Their drinks are healthier than ours --- a lot of fruit drinks. I tried a fresh mango drink the first day we were there and it was delicious! Here in America we seem to be more addicted to sodas and Starbucks.

At the deaf school the children were very supportive of each other, no matter their various disabilities and differing ages. They were very respectful of each other there. They also seem to be very resilient (more tough) and less spoiled. One of the Gallaudet students accidently hit a deaf student with a basketball. The student was about 8 years old. He did not cry, pout or complain. He just shrugged it off and continued playing. This impressed me as I think if the same thing had happened here in the U.S., the child probably would have gone running to an adult and wanted special care.

The children were very excited with the small gifts that we brought them. It took very little to make them happy. As I was watching them, I was thinking about how different it would have been if we had gone to a deaf school in the United States. I imagine students in the U.S. would have more likely been dissatisfied with their gifts. Maybe they'd want a different color, or wished they had gotten something another student received, or lost interest quickly.

b) What did you learn about yourself from this experience?

After spending a week in a totally different culture from the U.S., I realized how easily I adapted. I didn't miss the technology or the food or the comforts that we have back home. I was able to join in and be like them. Of course, I'm not sure if I could have done this long-term and on my own (without being with a large group of Americans), but I think I have the potential to join another culture and fit into their way of life.

I think my past experience, being born in Honduras and growing up there as a child, helped me to better understand the Costa Rican lifestyle. It also helped me to understand their frugal ways. They did not waste food. I noticed that they did a lot of recycling. They were more caring and respectful of their environment; recycling instead of creating waste or littering. I realize that I need to be more concerned about how we live in the United States. We are very wasteful here. We should follow more the attitudes that they have in Costa Rica about food and nature. Working with the children at the deaf school re-affirmed for me my desire to work with children in my future career. It was very inspiring and enjoyable to interact with them.

c) How did the trip change your attitudes, behaviors and perspectives as a global citizen?

One of the Gallaudet students in our group had to get around in a wheelchair. There were places that were hard to travel over and she needed help getting around. For example, it was impossible to wheel the chair around the sand on the beach. But several of us gladly helped her by carrying her and her chair so she could stay involved and keep up with the rest of us. It made me think, though, about how willing we are to help people like this girl when we are back home in the United States? When we were in Costa Rica, we had a different attitude. We were mentally prepared to help wherever we needed to help, and to help whoever needed our help. However, when we are back in our day-to-day lives, we don't have the same attitude.

That concerns me very much. I realize that I can act like two different people: indifferent (not really caring about others) when I am on the Gallaudet campus, but very caring and helpful when I am on a mission-type trip. This is not right, but probably happens with everyone. I would like to see myself as a caring and helpful person all the time, everywhere. So when I see a person in need, whether in Costa Rica, or on the Gallaudet campus, or anywhere else, I hope I remember what I learned from this experience and take the time to help that person out.

d) How did the trip influence you personally and academically?

From this experience in Costa Rica, I can see the value in traveling abroad and interacting with other cultures. If we never had the experience of seeing how other countries live, I can see us becoming very self-centered and only focusing on our own needs and desires. But from seeing how people in other parts of the world live, and what their values are, it pulls us outside of our own comfortable corner of the world. It makes us more aware of other people and broadens our understanding of life around the world. It also gives us ideas of how we might improve our own lives and futures, by learning from others.

Nori Rittenhouse   **March 25, 2012**

TODAY

Nori is a full-time student at Gallaudet University, the only university for the Deaf in the world. Recently Nori told me that from the time she heard about Gallaudet as a student at the Arkansas School for the Deaf, it was her dream to be a student there. She is majoring in Child and Family Studies and has three semesters remaining although she may stay an extra semester in order to do a second internship at Manos Felices in Tegucigalpa. How I would love to be a student at Manos Felices when Nori is there as a college student.

Nori also works in the campus post office and just recently she and her roommate Changer Gonzalez moved into an apartment (up until this move Nori had always lived on campus) near the university. Changer, from Rhode Island, is herself a graduate of Gallaudet. When Nori was home for a visit recently I asked her how many hours she would be carrying this fall term (fall 2012). When she told me "18-20", I advised her to take no more than 15 so as to allow time for fun. She said "Dad, I'm old. I've had my college fun. It's time for me to graduate and find a job." I tried to convince her otherwise until my wife Pat suggested that Nori was right where we'd hoped she'd be someday.

It seems that Nori is now on a mission of her own. God tends to take our experiences, including our sufferings, and turns them in to blessings for others if we are able to bend to His will. Nori's once dark and uncertain future now holds great hope for her and for those she touches. God's Hand of Favor will guide her future just as it always has. And some day God will pour out His Goodness on others through His emissary, Nori.

60

Printed in the United States
By Bookmasters